Composition for Young Musicians

A Fun Way for Kids to Begin Creating Music

Alfred, the leader in educational publishing, and the National Guitar Workshop, one of America's finest guitar schools, have joined forces to bring you the best, most progressive educational tools possible. We hope you will enjoy this book and encourage you to look for other fine products from Alfred and the National Guitar Workshop.

Jennifer Wilson

This book was acquired, edited and produced by Workshop Arts, Inc., the publishing arm of the National Guitar Workshop.
Nathaniel Gunod, managing and acquisitions editor
Burgess Speed, editor
Ante Gelo, music typesetter
Timothy Phelps, interior design
CD recorded at Jennifer Wilson's studio in Los Angeles, CA and Studio 9, Ontario, California.

Cover and interior photographs by Timothy Phelps.
Interior illustrations by Barbara Smolover.

ISBN 0-7390-3741-2 (Book & CD)

Alfred

Table of Contents

About the Author

Jennifer Wilson is an award winning composer who lives in Los Angeles, California. Her formal education includes a B.M. in Theory and Composition from the University of Western Ontario, and certificates in Piano Performance and Pedagogy from the Royal Conservatory of Music. She also received a post-graduate certificate in Scoring for Motion Pictures and Television from the University of Southern California. Studies with such luminaries as Henry Mancini and Jerry Goldsmith helped to further shape her understanding of how to create moods with music. In addition to film and television projects, Jennifer is involved in the development and use of new techniques and methodologies in music education.

PHOTO BY NAN HAGAN

Introduction

A Note to the Student

Anyone can compose music. It's fun—like making a painting, but with sound. You don't need to know any rules or how to play an instrument to do it. In fact, *you* will make up most of the rules!

In this book you will learn exciting ways to compose your own pieces at the piano (and other places too). You'll have the opportunity to try out lots of styles, create different moods and write down or draw your original music. There is a CD that goes with this book. It will help you understand how to do the exercises. It also has background sounds to use for your compositions to make them sound as great as they can!

A Note to Parents and Teachers

Beginning Composition for Kids supplies the basic tools to get your young composer started. It opens his/her mind, body, ears and eyes to sources of inspiration all around. A CD is included to inspire, explain, give demonstrations and provide colorful backgrounds for their musical compositions. They will also have the opportunity to write down or draw, in their own way, what their music sounds like to *them*. The goal is for the child to create and experience musical ideas without labels or analysis. The compositional process begins with a free expression of ideas and feelings and later evolves to the theory of structure and harmony.

Composition instruction reinforces regular piano lessons. It does this by encouraging students to make connections between what they are learning in performance and theory and what they are composing. This can give more meaning to their studies and also a deep sense of accomplishment.

How to Use the CD

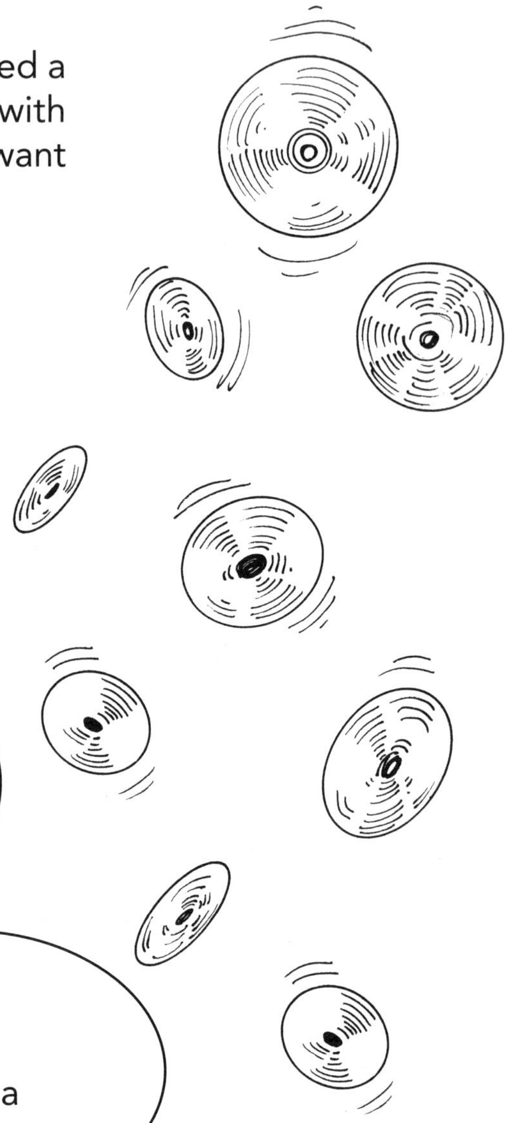

This book comes with a fun and easy-to-use CD. You will need a CD player near your keyboard so you can easily play along with the CD. Here are some ways you can set this up (you may want to ask your parents for help).

- A stereo in your keyboard room.
- A boom box next to your keyboard.
- A portable CD player with headphones.
- A computer CD player near your keyboard.

What you will hear...

Demonstrations

Clear demonstrations of everything in the book to help you make interesting choices in your compositions.

Games

Fun games to help you become a better composer.

Backgrounds

Colorful backgrounds to dress up your compositions. These backgrounds are fun to play along with and will help you learn to play with other instruments and sounds.

The CD that comes with this book can make learning easier and more enjoyable. The symbol to the left is next to the exercises and shows you which track to listen to.

Chapter One: Elements

"Creative people who know exactly what they're doing aren't creative people."

Anonymous

First Step to Composing

Composing is the art of organizing sounds into a musical piece—it is like thinking with sound.

Your first step in becoming a composer is to start noticing the sounds around you. Pay close attention to the sounds you enjoy and ask yourself why you like them. Do you like the whoosh of windshield wipers? Or the sound of water going down the drain? List a few of your favorite sounds below to the left. Also, think of some fun places where you would like to compose and list them below to the right.

My Favorite Sounds	Places to Compose Music
Windshield Wipers	At the park
Water going down drain	In the bathtub
	In a School Bus

Kitchen Instruments

It's amazing what "instruments" you can find in your own kitchen! Experiment by making sounds with a few *safe* objects. Invent your own instrument or try combining some of these:

- An empty jar
- An empty water bottle
- A metal bowl
- A pot
- A scouring brush
- A wooden spoon

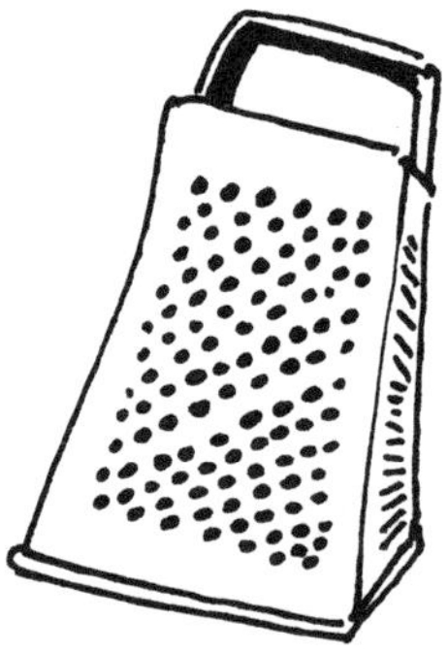

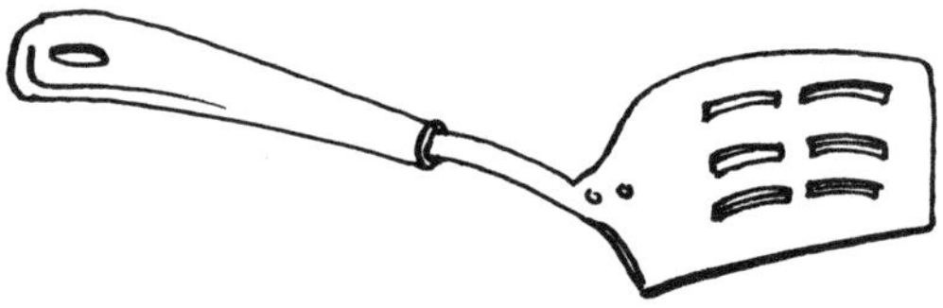

Remember:

Ask your parents for help. Be careful not to break anything or use anything that could be dangerous.

Listening and Playing Activity
On track 1 of your CD you will hear some short musical patterns. Using your kitchen instruments, imitate (play) each pattern after you hear it. When you're finished, play it again!

Pieces for Kitchen Instruments

When sounds are played in a pattern we can clap, it is called ***rhythm.*** There are all kinds of rhythms in music. Sometimes they feel steady like a heartbeat, and sometimes they dance about freely. Rhythms can be fast like the sound of horses galloping, and rhythms can be slow like a squeaky swing. You make rhythms all the time and don't even know it! Think about the last time you knocked on someone's door, went up a flight of stairs or even brushed your teeth!

Find a nice quiet place away from the piano to compose the following two pieces.

Kitchen Piece for One Person

- Using interesting rhythms, compose a piece on your kitchen instruments.

Listen for rhythms you make or hear today. What are they?

____

____

____

____

"All the sounds of the earth are like music."

Oscar Hammerstein (1895–1960)

Lyricist, writer and producer of musicals such as "The Sound of Music"

Kitchen Piece for Two People

- This piece is for you and a partner. You will use the rhythm instruments you made in the kitchen.
- Play short rhythms and ask your partner to copy you like an echo. Keep it simple so your partner can follow you easily. Have fun!

"Imagination is more important than knowledge."
Albert Einstein (1879–1955)
Scientist, philosopher, Nobel Prize winner

Piece for Black Keys

High—Low

Let's play the piano! When you play from one end of a keyboard to the other, you will pass through different ***ranges*** (areas of sound). At the far left, the range is low and dark and can almost sound like thunder. At the far right, the range is high and bright and almost sounds like bells or breaking glass. Each key on the piano makes a sound that has a particular ***pitch.*** Pitch tells you the highness or lowness of a musical sound or ***tone.*** Pitches get gradually higher as you move to the right on the piano.

Play random notes on your piano and listen for different pitches and ranges.

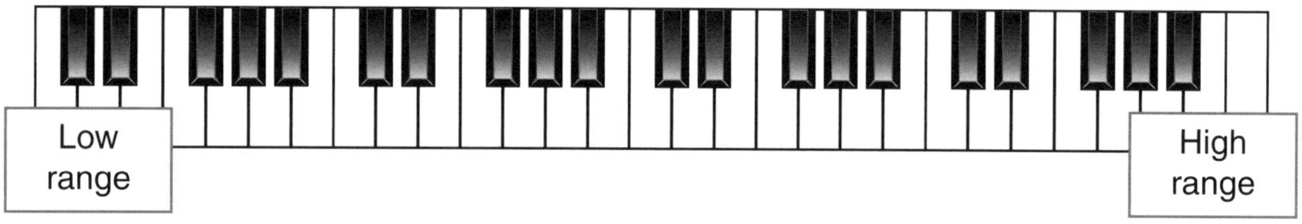

Story Form (A–B–A Form)

Music can be composed like a story, with a ***beginning, middle*** and ***end.*** Sometimes the beginning and end of a piece will sound the same, while the middle will sound different. We can use letters from the alphabet to show this.

A	B	A
Beginning	**Middle**	**End**

So another way to say ***story form*** is ***A–B–A form.***

Instructions:

1. For the beginning (A) section of your piece, make up some music on the black keys with your right hand.

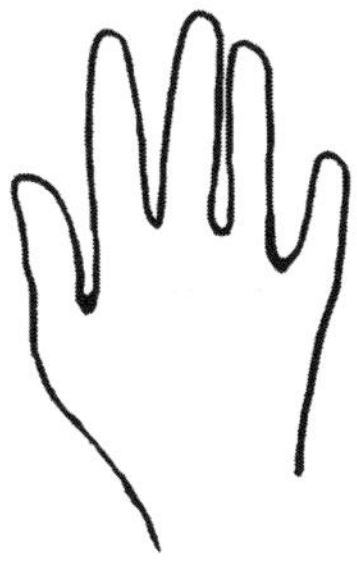

2. Next, compose a middle (B) section that sounds different than the A section. Use both hands at the same time on the black keys.

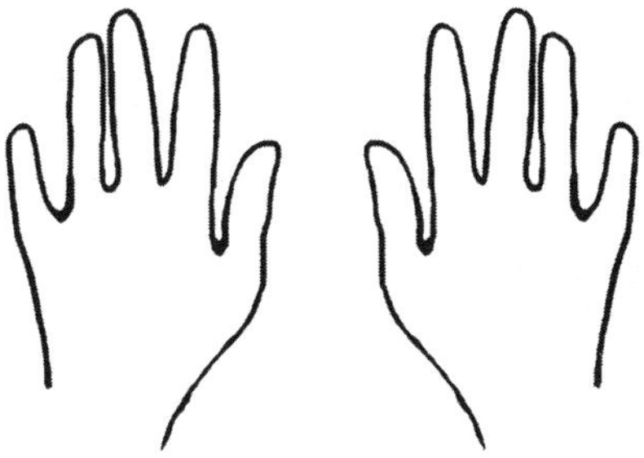

3. For the end (A) section, simply repeat the beginning!

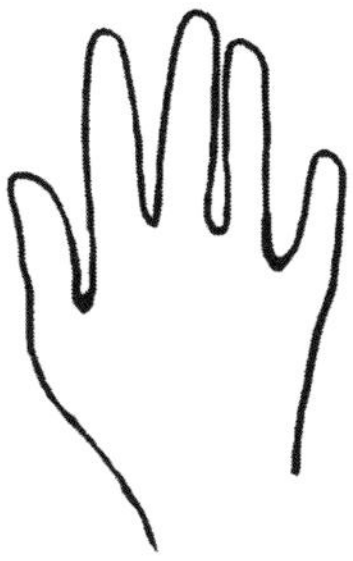

4. Now, play your piece with the background "soundscape" on track 2.

How did you make the B section sound different?

____

Composer's Quiz No. 1

(Answers: bottom of page 11.)

What is a "range?"

____

What is a "pitch?"

____

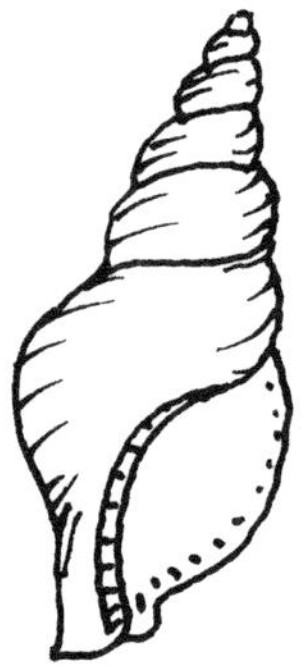

Repetition

Beautiful sounds are repeated in nature, like birdcalls and the ocean surf. In music, composers repeat elements they are attracted to. If you like it, play it again.

"The effects of good music are not just because it's new; on the contrary music strikes us more, the more familiar we are with it."

Johann Wolfgang von Goethe (1749–1832)

Writer, politician, humanist, scientist, philosopher

Not too **much**, not too little, just right.

Elements of music you can repeat:

- Pitches *Pitches Pitches Pitches*
- Rhythms *Rhythms*
- Patterns *Patterns Patterns*
- Moods *Moods Moods Moods*

Anything you can think of.

Repeating makes people listen, and makes music easier to remember.

Answers: page 10.

Pitch—The tone made by a key on a piano.

Range—An area of musical sound.

Cool Chords

Chords are fun and easy to play. A chord is three or more pitches, or keys on the piano, played at the same time. Chords are part of what makes us feel the mood of a song.

Making Chords

1. Using two fingers of your right hand and one finger of your left hand, play any three white keys at the same time. This is your first chord.

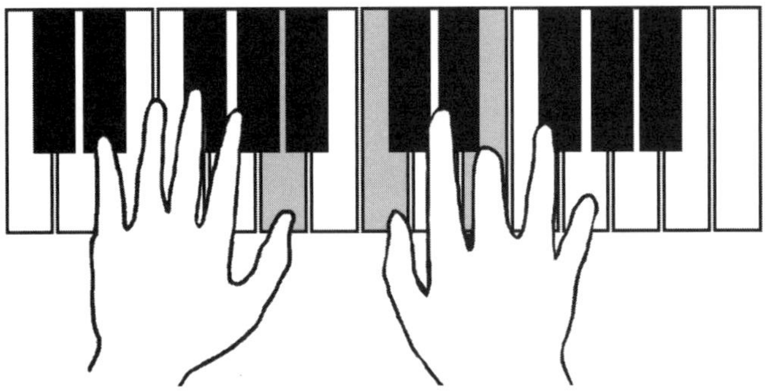

Keep your hands close together.

2. Now add another key that is close by, with a finger from either hand. This makes a new chord. It only takes one finger to make a new chord. In general, try not to move too many fingers at once.

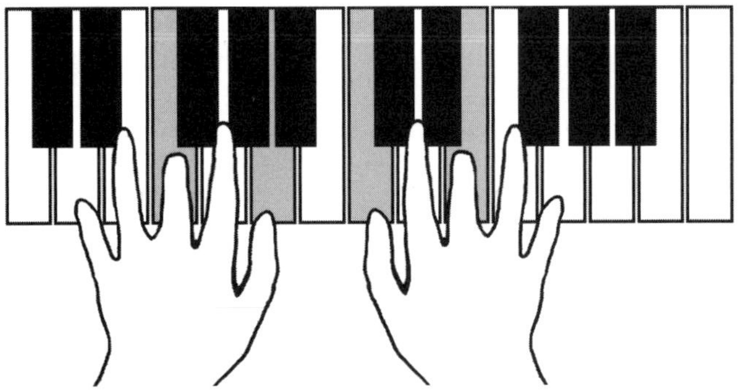

One finger can change a chord.

Making a Song

TRACK 3

1. Listen to the chords on track 3. Notice that they are played in a rhythm that goes with the ***beat*** of the music. In music, the beat is like a steady pulse or heartbeat. Notice that some of the chords are repeated.

TRACK 4

2. Play your own chords with the beat on track 4 and make up a song! Remember to use some chords more than once.

Composer's Quiz No. 2

(Answer: bottom of page.)

What is a "chord?"

____

____

Listening in Color

For this activity you will need:

- Several pieces of blank paper
- Colored pencils
- A few CDs (or the radio)

Instructions:

1. Listen to one of your favorite CDs. As you're listening, use colored pencils to draw whatever the music makes you feel.
2. Now get a fresh piece of paper. Listen to a different song, or piece of music, and with your colored pencils:
   - Move your hand from the left side of the paper to the right.
   - Make your hand move with the music.
   - Try to make your drawing look like what you are hearing. If the music goes up, make your hand go up. If the music goes down, make your hand go down.

TRACK 5

Here is a drawing of track 5. Listen to the CD to find out what it sounds like!

Answer: top of page.

Chord—Three or more pitches, or keys on the piano, played at the same time.

Score Layout

A ***score*** is a piece of music that is written down. There are many ways you can make a score. You can illustrate your music as a picture or write it on professional music paper. Either way, you should include the following information on your score.

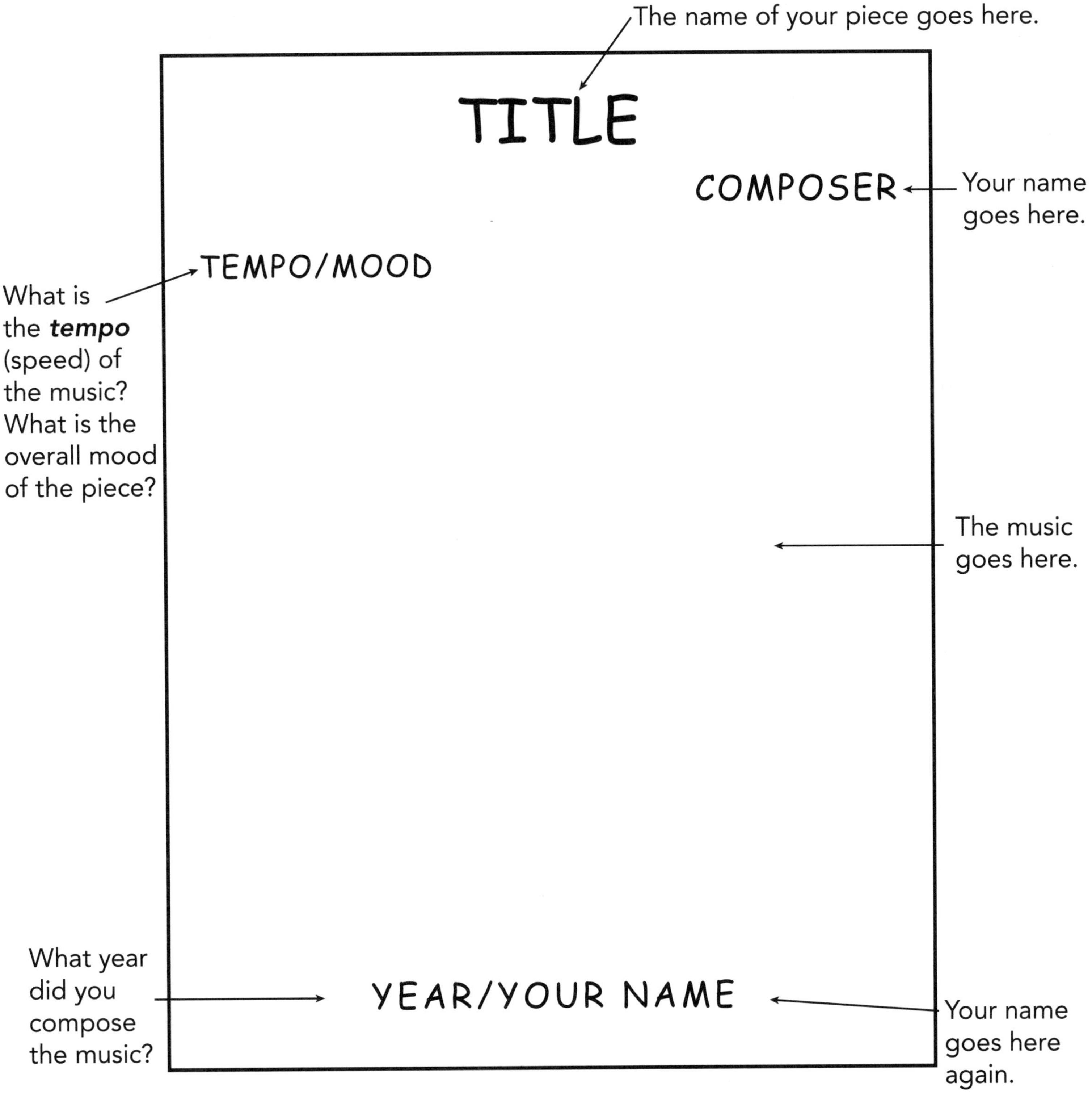

You could even turn the paper sideways if you want.

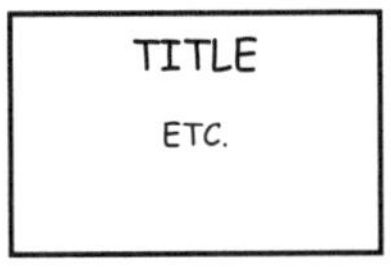

Make a Score

Compose a piece for the piano and illustrate (draw) it like a picture. Use colored pencils. Write words on the page telling how you want it to be played: fast, loud, quiet, etc. Have someone else try to play it!

Chapter Two: Moods

"Life is like music; it must be composed by ear, feeling, and instinct, not by rule."
Samuel Butler (1835–1902)
English writer and critic

anticipation

majestic CREEP silly HAPPY

Sweet hope

bounce gusto

glee calm brisk

Gallop empty

Loud and Quiet

There are many ways to add feeling to music. One of the most important ***devices*** (tools) to use is ***dynamics.*** Dynamics tell us how loud or quiet the music should be played. For example, "loud," "suddenly loud," "fading away," "very quiet," etc. Dynamics affect how the listener feels.

How would you feel if you heard:	**Describe the Dynamics**
A large dog barking at you?	
______________________________	____________________
Gentle rainfall?	
______________________________	____________________
The sudden screeching of car tires behind you?	
______________________________	____________________
A train fading away into the distance?	
______________________________	____________________
Your friends cheering for you?	
______________________________	____________________
Nothing?	
______________________________	____________________

Moody 5ths

5ths can be used to create all kinds of beautiful moods. For example, you can create in sound an ancient world, a magic forest or a joyful dance.

A 5th is the distance between five white keys (or eight keys when counting white and black keys). They are easy to play with one hand. Use fingers 1 and 5 (thumb and little finger). You can play the two keys at the same time or you can play them separately.

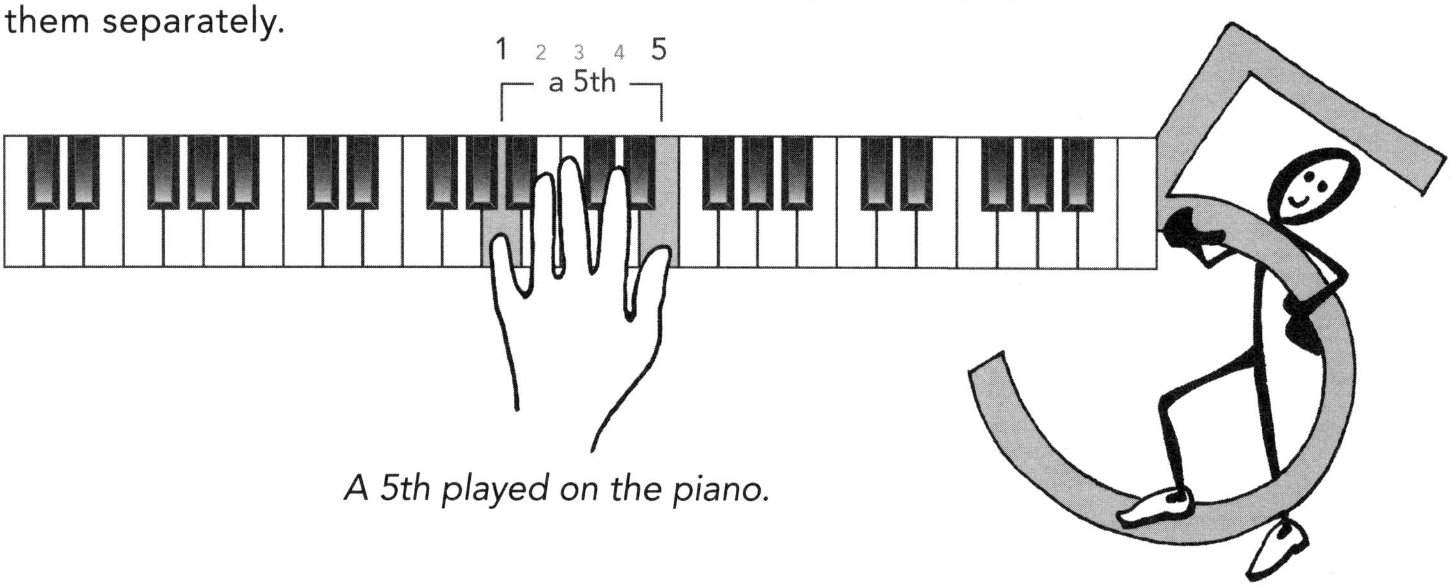

A 5th played on the piano.

Try this!

- With your left hand, play a 5th using white keys. Do not play it too loudly.
- Now move the same hand to a different 5th.
- And then another...

There's a lot you can do with these moody sounds!

Instructions:

Using your left hand, play 5ths along with track 6.
Do your best to:

- Hold some 5ths longer than others.
- Create a calm mood by playing quietly.
- Repeat the 5ths that sound best to you.

Expressive Words

Composers often write a word or two on their scores to describe the mood they want played.

Examples of words to describe moods:

Calm

Longing

Excited

Joyful

In as few words as possible, describe some moods you created using 5ths.

____

____

____

____

The Haunted Piano

TRACK 7

It's time to write a creepy story about a haunted piano. Make sure your story has one or two scary surprises in it. Listen to track 7 while you write it. Add pictures too!

Scary Music

Compose some scary music (like movie music) to go with your story about the haunted piano on page 20.

How to Compose Scary Music

- Use **black keys and white keys at the same time.** If you play only white keys or only black keys, your piece will sound too pretty.
- Use **repetition.** Play a few notes, wait, and then play them again. Waiting in between makes the audience wonder what will happen next.
- Create a scary **surprise** by suddenly getting **loud!**
- Play in different **ranges** (page 8) on the keyboard: high, middle and low.

- Create your music while listening to the **sound effects** on track 7.

Put It All Together!

1. Ask someone to read your story aloud.

2. While they read your story, play your scary music on the piano along with track 7.

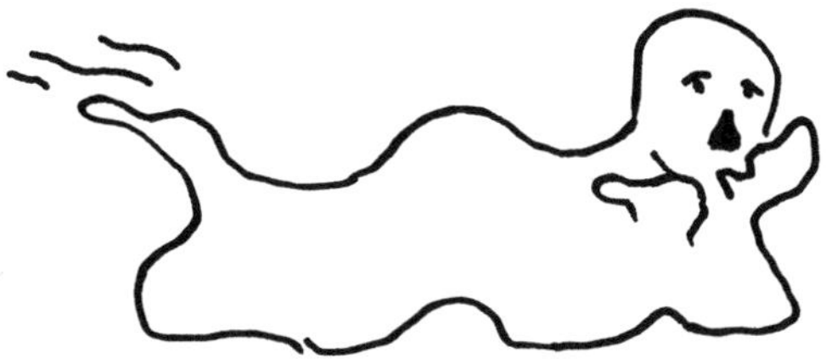

"A note of music gains significance from the silence on either side."
Anne Morrow Lindbergh (1906–2001)
American pioneer in aviation, author, poet

Silence

In music we call silence a ***rest.*** Silence...
creates suspense and
makes the audience
listen more closely.

Foreground and Background

Music can be composed like a picture, with some things in the ***foreground*** *(front),* and other things in the ***background*** (back). In art, the objects in the background usually blend into each other; in music, the background is usually quiet.

Background Ostinato

In music, an effective way to create a background is to use an ***ostinato.*** An ostinato is a few notes that repeat over and over. It can almost seem to blend into the background.

Activity

1. Ostinato 1—In the middle range of the piano, pick three white keys that are close together. Play them quietly over and over. To help blend the sound, use the ***sustain pedal***. This is the foot pedal to the right on your piano that makes the tones last after you have taken your fingers off the keys. Listen to the example on track 8.

2. Ostinato 2—In the high range of the piano, pick three white keys that are far apart. Play them very quietly, over and over. Use the pedal to blend the sound. Experiment! Listen to track 9 for an example of this.

Echo Echo Echo Echo

Let's explore ***imitation,*** or copying—a very important device in music. Just like in nature, an echo in music can be a short bit of sound that is quietly repeated.

Instructions:

1. Imagine you are somewhere outside where you can hear an echo. Maybe you're in a beautiful canyon surrounded by majestic cliffs.

2. On the piano, compose a short bit of music with your left hand. Wait a second, and then echo it quietly with your right hand in a higher range.

TRACK 10

3. Compose three more bits of music and echo them like you did with the first. Listen to track 10 for examples.

4. Sketch (draw) your echo music any way you'd like to.

"Creativity takes courage." Henri Matisse (1869–1954)
French painter, sculptor and philosopher

Tune

A ***tune*** is the part of a song that we sing. Did you know that a ***melody*** and a tune are the same thing?

Steps

In music, tunes can move in ***steps.*** Steps are small. A ***whole step*** is the distance between two piano keys that have one key in between. Sometimes the key in between will be black, sometimes it will be white.

Try this. Pick a white key. Go to the next white key. As long as there is one key in between, you've taken a step!

A ***half step*** is the distance of two keys that have no keys in between them.

If you want to compose a tune that is easy to sing and play, use ***stepwise motion,*** which happens when you move in whole steps and half steps.

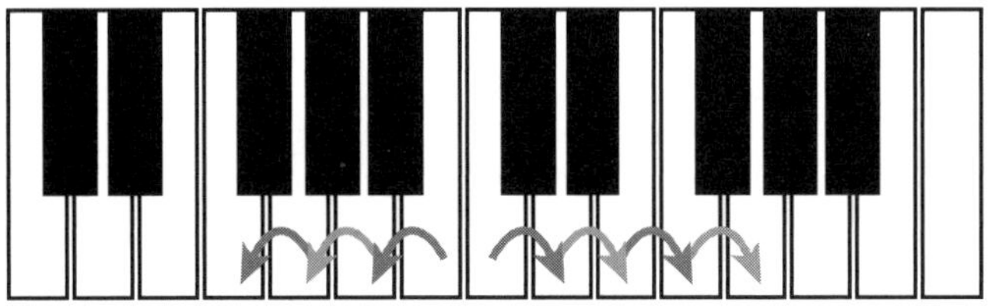

Stepwise Motion.

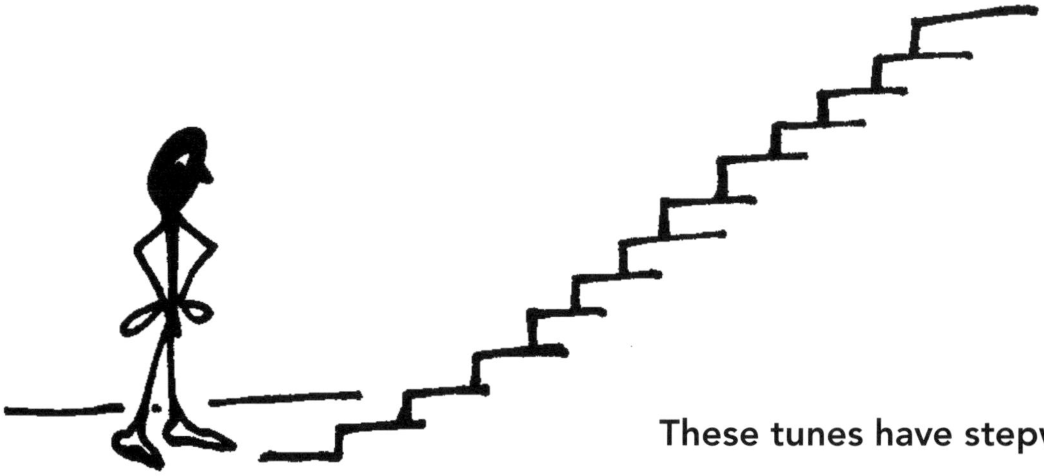

These tunes have stepwise motion:

"This Land Is Your Land"

"Ode to Joy"

"Jingle Bells"

"Yankee Doodle"

"Yesterday"

Leaps

Sometimes there will be ***leaps*** in a tune. A leap happens when you skip over two or more keys to get where you're going. Leaps can make a tune interesting, but be careful—*lots* of leaps in one direction can make it more difficult to sing or play.

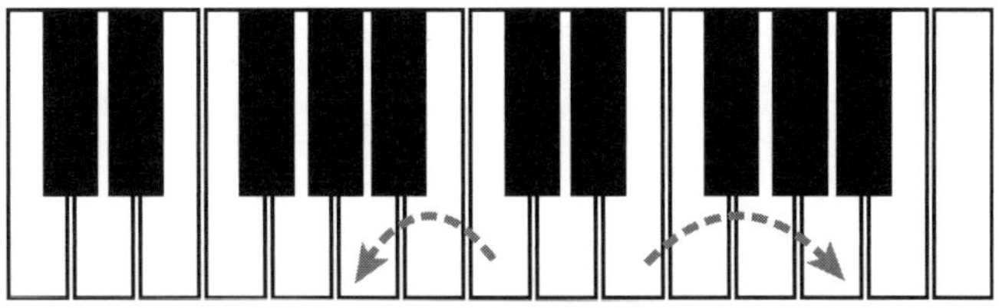

Small Leap. Bigger Leap.

Let's make a tune!

Instructions:

TRACK 11

1. On the white keys, play a tune with the music you hear on track 11. Use stepwise motion and only a few leaps.
2. Repeat some of your tune to make it easier to remember.

"Do not fear mistakes. There are none."
Miles Davis (1926–1991)
American jazz composer, trumpeter, bandleader

Improvising

When musicians make up what they're playing—as they play it—it is called ***improvisation.***

Let's try improvising. It's fun! First you need to find ***middle C***. On your keyboard, notice that the black keys are grouped in twos and threes. Find the group of two black keys in the middle of the keyboard. To the left of these is a white key called middle C.

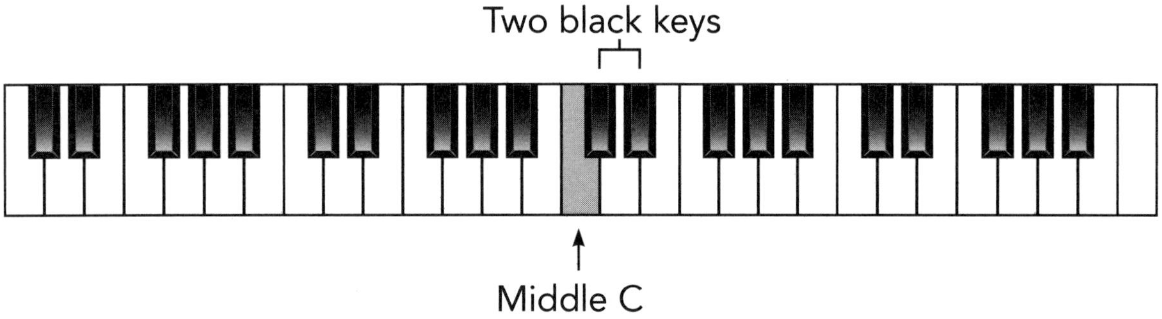

Instructions:

Using only your thumb (either one) on middle C, improvise to the music on track 12.

Improvising Hint
Play a combination of long tones, short tones and silences. You'll sound like a professional!

Make Phrases

A ***phrase*** is a short musical statement that has a beginning, middle and end.

To make a phrase, play a combination of long tones, short tones and silences.

Let's add two more pitches to your improvisation: $\boldsymbol{E^{\flat}}$ (pronounced "E-flat") and ***F***. Use the illustration below to find them on your keyboard.

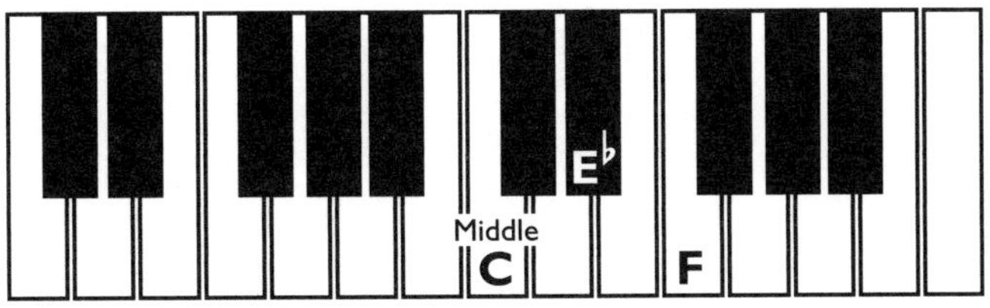

Instructions:

Use the three pitches (middle C, $E^{\flat}$ and F) to play along again with track 12.

- Play phrases.
- Repeat them.
- Change them slightly.
- Play them at different tempos (speeds).

Have fun!

Winter Snow

Let's get into a winter mood. Write down some things that are snowy and cold.

Icicles	__________	__________
Snowflakes	__________	__________
__________	__________	__________

TRACK 13

Now it's time to compose a winter piece using A–B–A form (see page 8). For a wintry touch, try making sleigh bells on the piano. It's easy! Play a group of three white keys in a row, at the same time, in the high range. Listen to track 13 for an example.

Instructions:

1. For your A section, play only white keys (like snow) in the middle and high ranges of your piano. Use your sustain pedal.

TRACK 14

   - With one hand, compose a wintry ostinato (see page 22). Use only three or four notes that repeat. Listen to track 14 for an example.
   - With the other hand, play long sustained notes. Play them one by one or in 5ths (page 18), both keys at the same time.

TRACK 15

2. Next, compose a B section, again using the white keys. Make it different from the A section. For example, play fast notes in stepwise motion for a sound like glistening bells and icicles. Or change ranges with one or both hands. Again, use the sustain pedal. Listen to track 15 for inspiration.

TRACK 15

3. Play your piece with track 15.

Composer's Quiz No. 3

(Answer: bottom of page 29.)

What is a musical "phrase?"

____

____

Now illustrate (draw) the piece you composed on page 28, showing the A–B–A form.

A

B

A

Answer: page 28.

Phrase—A short musical statement that has a beginning, middle and end.

Standard Music Notation

Standard music notation is a way of writing music that communicates exact pitch and rhythm and can be used for all instruments. You may already be learning about this in your regular music lessons. It can help you to be very clear about what you want played.

The Treble Clef Staff

A ***staff*** has five lines and four spaces. The ***treble clef*** symbol 𝄞 is at the beginning of the staff and tells us the music is written for the right hand (or another ***treble*** or high-pitched instrument such as the flute or violin).

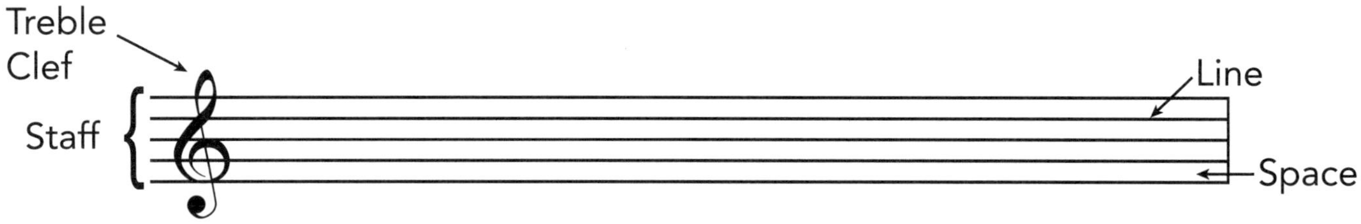

Notes

Music is written by placing ***notes*** 𝅝 on a staff. The pitch of a note is shown by *where* it is placed (which line or space) on the staff. When a note is too high or low for the staff, it is placed on its own line called a ***ledger line***. The note for middle C is on the first ledger line under the treble clef staff.

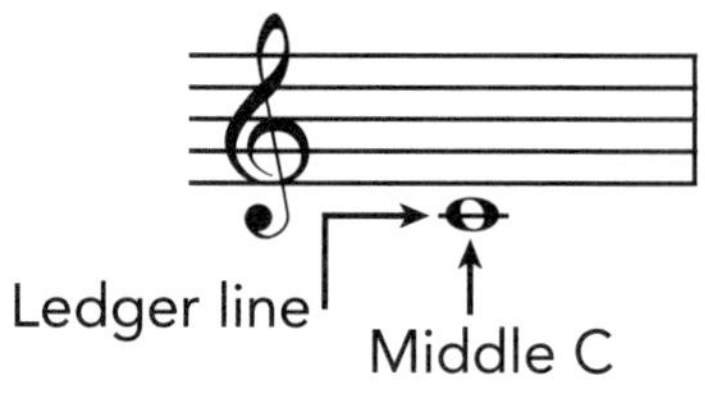

Let's write a middle C. Make a ledger line under the staff. Now draw the round note, with the ledger line going through its middle. Then make a row of middle Cs.

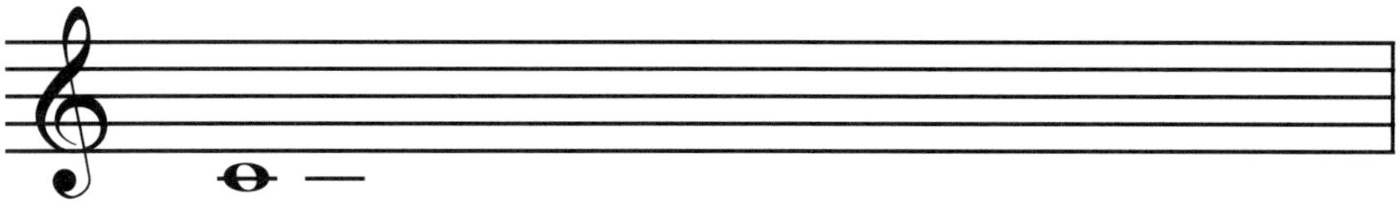

Now find middle C on your keyboard, just like you did when you were improvising (page 26). Play it while looking at the written notes. This will help you get used to how it looks and sounds.

Note Lengths

Music is measured in ***beats.*** The beats create a steady pulse that is like a heartbeat. Some notes are short and last for one beat. Other notes are longer and last for two or even four beats. How a note looks tells you how long it lasts.

Quarter note.
It is *short* and gets 1 beat.

Half note.
It is *longer* and gets 2 beats.

Whole note.
It is the *longest* and gets 4 beats.

How to draw a quarter note:

1. First make a ***note head***
2. Fill it in
3. Add a ***stem***

Draw

A *quarter* note ______ A *half* note ______ A *whole* note ______

Rest Lengths

Remember, rests (page 22) are silences in music.

A ***quarter rest*** gets 1 beat of silence.

A ***half rest*** gets 2 beats of silence.

A ***whole rest*** gets 4 beats of silence.

Composer's Quiz No. 4
(Answers: bottom of page 32.)

Under each note or rest, write the number of beats it gets.

Piece for Middle C

Instructions:

1. Take your book and find a place away from the piano to compose. Compose a piece using middle C only. Think of one-note sounds in nature (like drops of water, or a woodpecker). Close your eyes and imagine how one note could be interesting. Use different note and rest lengths. Go fast, go slow, play loud, play quiet, etc.

2. Write your piece on the treble clef staff.

3. Add descriptive words telling how you want the music to be played.

   Examples:

   Get faster

   Bouncy

   Quiet

   Get louder here

4. Don't forget to give your piece a title and sign your name.

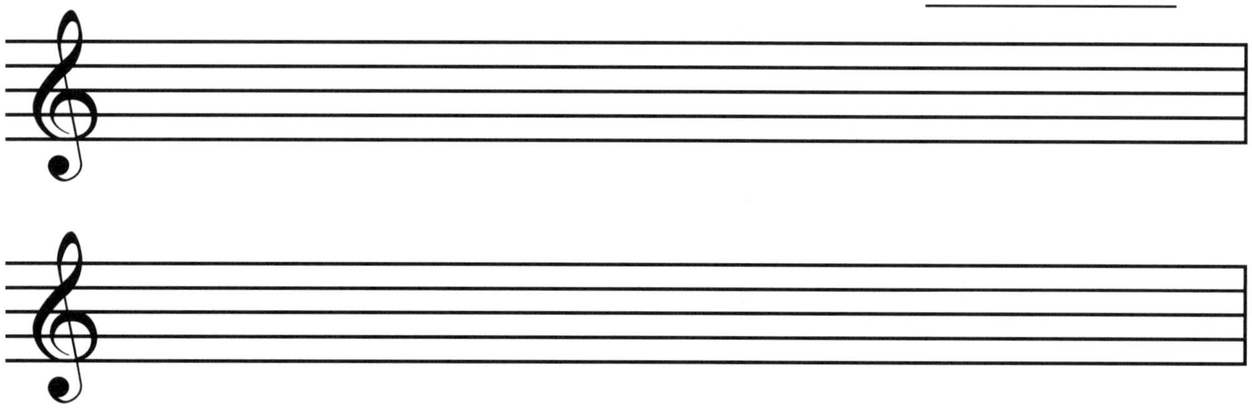

5. Now play your piece!

Answers: page 31.

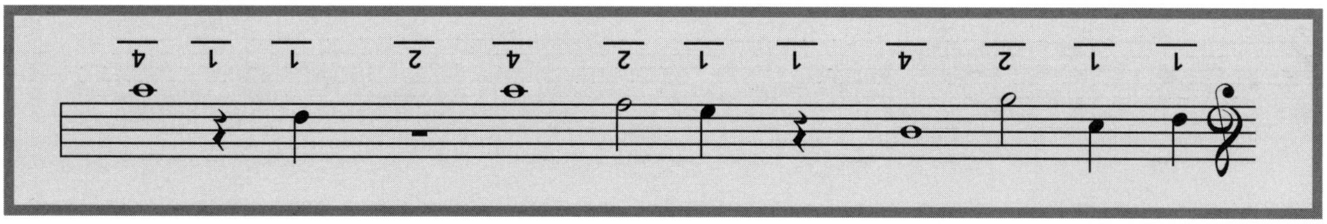

Chapter Three: Design

"Music is the art of thinking with sounds."
Jules Combarieu (1859–1916), Author

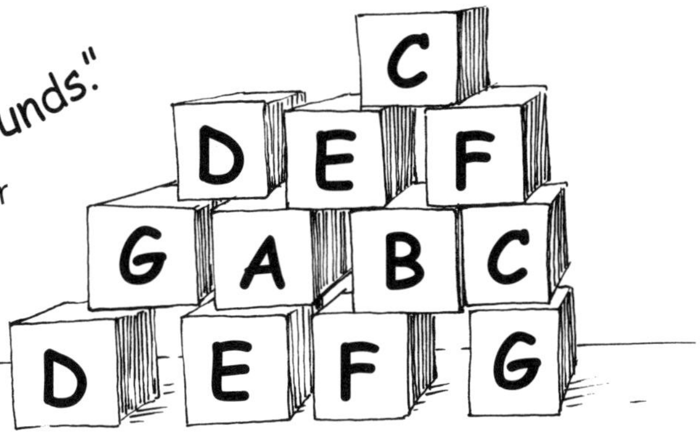

Finding C–D–E–F–G–A–B

There are just seven white keys on the piano. Only seven?! Well, seven *differently-named* white keys. They repeat in a pattern just like the black keys do. Each key has its own letter-name from the ***musical alphabet*** (A–B–C–D–E–F–G). The letter-names go in alphabetical order and repeat after G. You can start with any letter. Let's look at the musical alphabet on the keyboard starting with C.

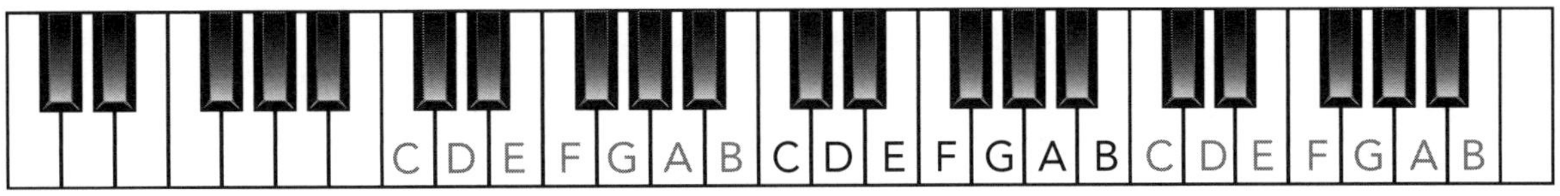

Playing Words on the Keyboard

1. Play "D–A–D."
2. Play "B–A–G."
3. Play "F–A–C–E."
4. In a different range, play "B–A–D–G–E."
5. Play "C–A–B–B–A–G–E."

Which musical words do you like best? ______________________

Can you compose a piece using words? ______________________

Do you have musical letters in your name? ______________________

Composer's Quiz No. 5
(Answers: bottom of page 34.)

1. Which white keys have you learned so far in this book?

   ____

2. Which white key is between the group of two black keys? __________

3. Which white key is just to the left of the three black keys? __________

Writing C–D–E–F–G–A–B

Notes on the staff go stepwise (page 24, Steps) on lines and spaces. They alternate: line note–space note–line note, etc.

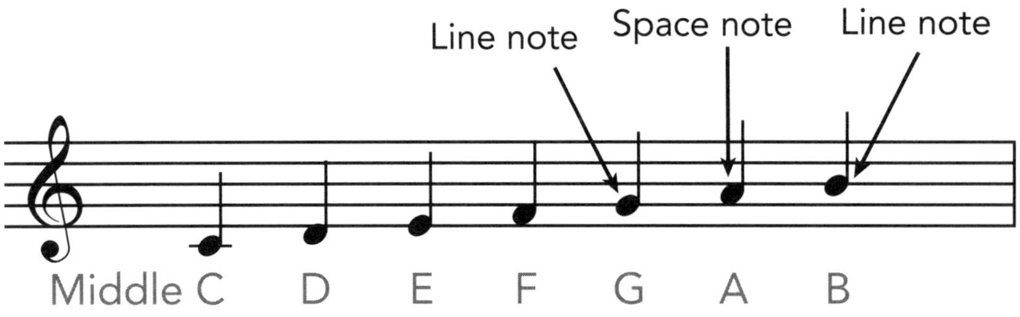

Find the letters to make these words on the staff to the left!

- Bag
- Face
- Cab

Composer's Quiz No. 6
(Answers: bottom of page 35.)

Look at the staff above. Which notes are:

Space notes? ______________________________

Line notes? ______________________________

Instructions:

1. Trace each note head; fill it in black; trace the ledger line and stem (the line going up from the note).
2. Write the note names underneath.
(Answers: bottom of page 35.)

__ __ __ __ __ __ __

Answers: page 33.

1. C–D–E–F–G–A–B 2. D 3. F

Music Jumble

Instructions:

1. Play the music you see below. (Write the note names underneath the music if that makes it easier for you.) Do you hear or see phrases? Can you see patterns that repeat?

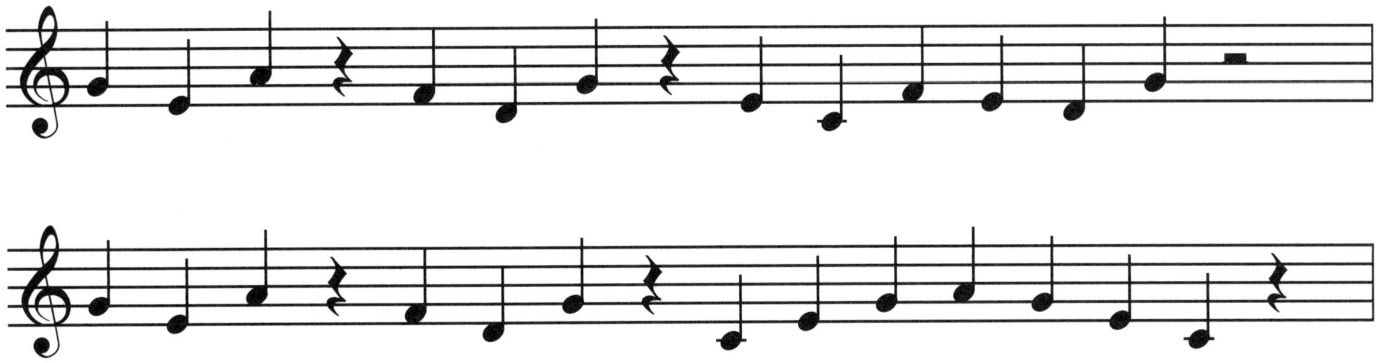

2. Neatly copy this music onto a new piece of music paper. Use a pencil!

3. Take the music you just copied and cut it into four sections.

4. Now jumble the sections into a new order and play it! Turn some sections upside down to see what they look like. Jumble them again.

5. Choose the way you like best and paste it below.

All Answers: page 34.

Space notes: D–F–A

Line notes: C–E–G–B

Note names from note-tracing exercise: C–D–E–F–G–A–B

Chance Music

Believe it or not, many composers have used chance, or luck, to compose. The fancy name for this kind of music is ***aleatoric,*** which is derived from the word "alea" (dice) and means "in any order" or "done randomly." For this piece you will need one die (that's one of two dice) and a coin. (If you don't have a die, put six pieces of paper—numbered 1 through 6—into a hat.)

Instructions:

1. The roll of the die will decide which notes you will use. Each of the six numbers on the die will stand for a note: 1=C, 2=D, 3=E, 4=F, 5=G, 6=A.

   Ready? Roll the die. Good luck!

1	2	3	4	5	6	(die roll)
C	D	E	F	G	A	(note to be used)

   Which note did you get? ____________________

2. A flip of the coin will decide the note's ***value*** (length). If you get "heads," it is a quarter note; "tails" is a half note.

   Ready? Toss the coin.

Heads = Quarter note	♩
Tails = Half note	𝅗𝅥

   What note length did you get? _______________

3. Next, write this note with its correct value at the beginning of the staff below.

4. Continue to add notes by rolling the die and flipping the coin until you reach the end of the music staff. If you like, keep going onto the second staff.

5. Now, play your chance music! Use the sustain pedal. For fun, try playing both ***staves*** (more than one staff) at the same time.

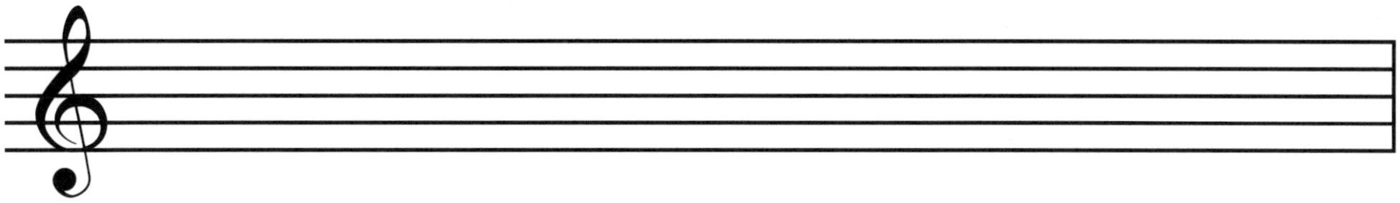

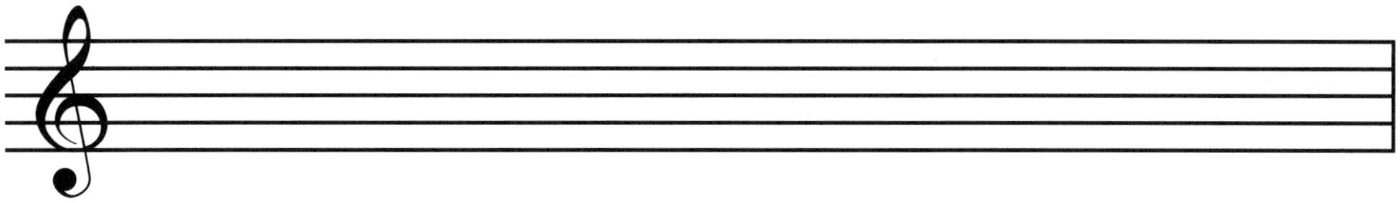

"Great artists have an element of chance in their talent, and there is also talent in their chance."

Victor Hugo (1802–1885), French author and poet

Animal Themes

In music, a ***theme*** (which rhymes with dream) is one of the main musical ideas or phrases of a piece. We hear music themes all the time. Characters in movies often have their own musical theme. Can you think of some? Hedwig? Batman? The Lion King? Jaws?

An animal theme can be short. It can express the character of the animal with just a few notes. Listen to the examples.

A charming snake.

A grumpy bear.

A merry squirrel.

Instructions:

1. Compose a short musical theme for each of these animals:

   A fidgety frog.

   A funny elephant.

   A dizzy bumblebee.

   Try to capture the animal's character. Consider the questions below:

   - How do they move? Are they fast? Slow? Heavy and clumsy? Do they jump? Dance?
   - What size are they? Big? Small?
   - What sounds do they make? Are they loud? Quiet? Scary? Squeaky?

2. In the space below, write a story about these animals. Feel free to add others from your imagination, or from a show or book you like.

3. Now have someone read your story aloud. Each time one of the animals is mentioned, play its musical theme.

Theme and Variations

You learned that a theme is an important musical phrase or idea. A ***variation*** is that same theme *changed* in some way. Easy!

Ways to change a theme into a variation:

- Change some of the notes.
- Play the theme in a different range.
- Play the theme faster or slower.
- Add something funny.
- Add some chords or 5ths with the other hand.
- Change the mood by playing it quieter or louder.

TRACK 19

Listen to track 19 to hear an example of a theme and two variations.

Instructions:

1. Compose a short, simple theme. This is what you play first.
2. Compose two variations. Use ideas from the list above or invent some of your own.
3. See if you can write your theme on the staff with notes you've learned. It doesn't have to be perfect. Write it any way you can to help you remember it.
4. Illustrate your two variations below your theme in a way that helps you best remember them. You can draw them, use note names, draw a staff or use any combination of these.

Theme and Variations Piece

Theme

Variation 1

Variation 2

"The best way to have a good idea is to have a lot of ideas."
Linus Pauling (1901–1994)
Scientist, humanitarian, Nobel Prize winner

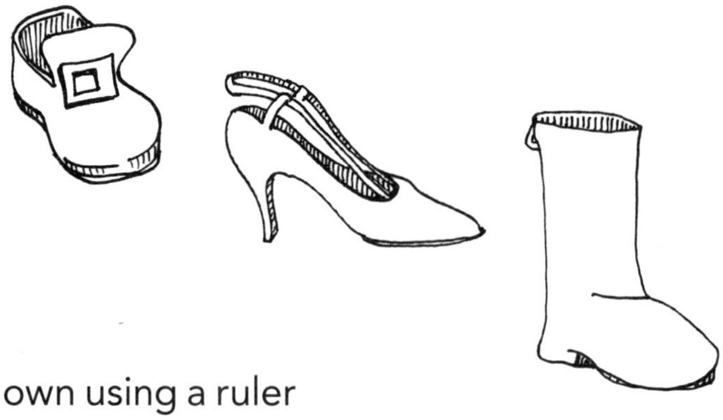

Shoebox Piece

This is a fun piece! You will need:

- A shoebox (or some kind of container)
- Music paper (store-bought, or make your own using a ruler or straight edge)
- Scissors

The music will be in ***through-composed*** form, which means it will be continuous, without repeating itself. It will take six days in a row to compose. Each day, you will add a little bit of music without looking at what you wrote the day before.

Instructions:

Day 1 — Checklist

1. Compose a short phrase (about four to eight notes long). ______
   - Use notes you have learned: C–D–E–F–G–A–B.
   - Use quarter notes, half notes, whole notes and rests.
2. Neatly write the phrase on music paper. ______
3. Clip out the music with scissors. Label it "Day 1" and put it in the shoebox. Have Mom or Dad keep your shoebox for you. Don't peek! ______

Days 2–5

1. Each day compose a new short phrase without looking at what's already in the shoebox.
2. Clip out each day's music, label it and put it in the shoebox.

Day 6

1. Open the shoebox!
2. Take out all the clippings. Arrange them from 1 to 5 and play them.

Neatly paste your piece below.

"The only thing better than singing is more singing."

Ella Fitzgerald (1917–1996)

Jazz singer, Grammy award winner, dubbed "The First Lady of Song"

Song

TRACK 20

Which comes first when composing a song—the music or the words? What do *you* think? Start with either, or write them at the same time—you're the composer! On track 20, there is some music to which you will add words and a melody. Listen to this track now.

Instructions:

1. Make a list of things that are important to you. Some examples might be: being a good friend, your love of nature, something you find funny, or even a favorite place you like to go.

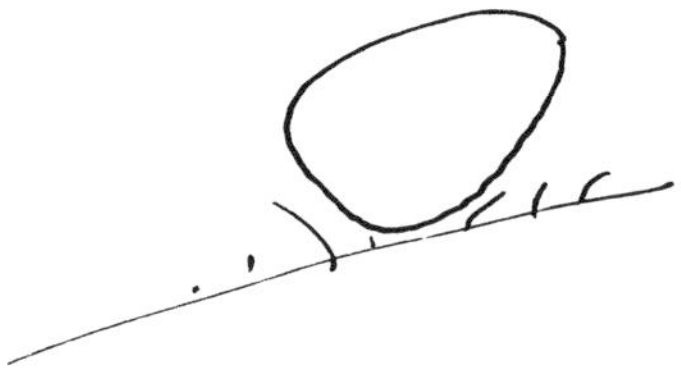

Your song will be in ***simple song form.***

- Simple song form has an A section ***(verse)*** and a B section ***(chorus)***. A verse is the part of a song that tells a story and changes with each repetition. The chorus is the part of the song that repeats after each verse.
- The sections are arranged in this way: **A–B–A–B–B.**

2. Next, use your list of important things to come up with words for your song.

Title ____________________

Your Name ____________________

Verse I Tell us something—a story. Use short sentences. Try rhyming.

____
____
____
____

Chorus This is the most important part of the song. Say something important in only a few words and repeat, repeat!

____
____
____
____

Verse II Continue your story. Tell us more!

____
____
____
____

Chorus Now repeat the chorus.

Chorus Repeat the chorus again.

3. Finally, sing your words along with track 20, making up the tune as you go.

Free Piece

Compose any kind of piece you want. You make the rules!

- Make it at least 30 seconds long.
- Illustrate and/or ***notate*** (write the notes for) your piece in the space below.
- Give it a title and put your name and date on it.

Congratulations!

Few people attempt to explore the mysteries of composition and you have just completed your first body of work as a composer! Take good care of it as a keepsake of your early pieces and a record of your progress as a beginning composer.

This book has made you aware of the elements of music and has given you valuable tools to express yourself in new ways. But it's just the beginning. Discover the music within you and let it sing!

"There is nothing greater than the joy of composing something oneself and then listening to it."

Clara Schumann (1819–1896)

Composer, virtuoso pianist